STILL IRISH

For Jack Ryan —
Belmont's only fun-loving, soccer-playing,
movie-going leprechaun —
the man with the big heart —
this a second time !
Kevin Rochett
May '96

STILL IRISH

a century of the Irish in film

WRITTEN BY KEVIN ROCKETT

PICTURE RESEARCH BY EUGENE FINN, KEVIN ROCKETT

RED MOUNTAIN PRESS - DUBLIN

This book is dedicated to the memory of Tiernan MacBride who died in July 1995.

Published by

Red Mountain Press Limited

23 Clarinda Park West

Dún Laoghaire

Ireland

Text copyright © Kevin Rockett 1995

Picture selection copyright © Red Mountain Press Limited 1995

Designed by Paul Rattigan at Zeus

Printed by Impress Printing Works

ISBN 1 900361 00 0

Acknowledgements: The publishers would like to thank those film production and distribution companies whose publicity stills appear in this book. Thanks also to the staff of the British Film Institute Stills, Posters and Designs Department; National Film and Television Archive, Berkhamstead; Markuu Salmi, Library and Information Services, British Film Institute; Liam Wylie, Irish Film Archive; National Film and Sound Archive, Canberra; Film Ireland; Pat Dawson, John McCarthy and the Trustees of Muckross House, Killarney, Co Kerry; Michelle Cooper-Galvin; Dairena Ní Chinnéide; Herbert Reynolds; Robert Monks; Eibhlís Ní Dhuibhne, National Library of Ireland; Leni McCullagh, Radio Telefís Éireann.

CONTENTS

INTRODUCTION

As national cinemas worldwide celebrate both the national and international character of the cinema during its centenary year, the film stills collected here represent the diverse range of films made about the Irish. The nature of national cinemas are the subject of debate at present, especially as to the relative balance between their 'national' and 'international' character. This debate has been as intense in Ireland as elsewhere. One of the main impediments to the development of a distinctive Irish cinema has been the imbalance between the budgets available to indigenous and foreign productions. At a cultural level, though, the very notion of 'Irishness' has been broadened in recent years to incorporate more completely the wide Irish diaspora. This has been no less true in the cinema than in other areas of cultural activity. While less than one hundred feature films have been made by Irish film-makers in Ireland during the cinema's first century, more than two thousand fiction films have been produced about the Irish outside the country. The stills included here are designed to give due weight to that fact.

The freezing of space and time, the very antithesis of cinema, is the preserve of film stills photography, but these apparently ephemeral moments may linger in a culture for decades after a film has left the cinemas. The still photograph will retain the trace not just of the film, but of the real life stars which it is promoting, and the culture and society, the social class, ethnic group or gender represented in the film. Our memory of particular historical periods may be anchored by these still images and our interpretation of events may be determined by the representation of a mood or a character in a film, or in a film still. When a film is long forgotten, it is often only the still image which remains in people's memory and, if the film has not been preserved in an archive, it may be the only surviving visual record of the film. There are, regrettably, a number of films in the following pages for which no copy of the film has so far been re-discovered. Only the still survives.

RYAN'S DAUGHTER
(David Lean, GB, 1970, colour)

Film stills are produced for publicity and promotional purposes, and such images are used for graphics on posters, advertisements and handbills. To this end, Hollywood studios employed over three hundred stills photo- graphers during its classical period from the 1920s to the 1950s. The purpose of all this effort was, of course, to encourage people to pay to see the film. Even in Hollywood's classical period, it was unlikely that a stills photographer was permanently on set. Choices were made not just about which scenes would be photographed and promoted, but about the version of that scene which would be frozen for the photographer. A stills photographer may 'shoot through the lens', replicating the scene which the moving camera is taking. As likely, though, the stills photographer would shoot from another angle of the set, and thus give a different effect to the scene. 'Tableaux' which 'summarised' a scene or the film itself would also be arranged for the stills photographer. Additionally, posed portraits of the stars by themselves, or with the lead male and female stars in an embrace, were widely used for promotional purposes. In its concentration on narrative moments as used by publicists, such non-narrative stills are not included in this book.

The factory-like work of the Hollywood studios, with their precise division of labour and their continuity of production, which provided for the employment of renowned stills photographers, is an economic world away from non-American film-making. Whether in Europe or Australia, the two areas besides America covered by this book, film budgets do not usually allow for the production values we normally associate with the classical American cinema. Therefore, one of the difficulties in selecting stills for this book is the obvious visual power of American stills vis-a-vis their British, Australian and Irish counterparts. In general, these latter stills do not carry the same visual impact as their American counterparts. Indeed, it is only in recent years that Irish film-makers working within an indigenous tradition have had budgets which allowed for the occasional employment of a stills photographer. As a result, there are many key films from Irish cinema history for which no stills, no frozen 'summary', exists.

STOP THIEF! (Gerard Healy, Ireland, 1953, b&w)
Cameraman George Fleischmann photographs a drama documentary on children's health.

This book seeks to link thematically the recurring narrative motifs in Irish cinema and the cinemas of the Irish diaspora, a term used here to designate those countries, especially the USA, Great Britain and Australia which were the destinations of large numbers of Irish migrants. For the purposes of this book, and of its reference companion, *The Irish Filmography* by Kevin Rockett, which is published in 1996, some continental European films are also included.

Given Ireland's long struggle for independence and the continuing conflict over the political partition of the island, it is not surprising that Irish history and politics, the subject of chapter one, should occupy a central place in cinema images of Ireland. Migration from Ireland to America and Australia, chapter two, has been a voluntary and involuntary feature of Irish life for centuries. The act of migration, with its pain of separation and the difficulties of settling in the new country, has been balanced in the cinema by the positive features of the new life. Often using comedy, American cinema sought to represent the cultural diversity of the new country and to explore the processes of integration. One of the central elements of life in Ireland as well as in the new territories was the struggle for the land and of work in general, the subject of chapter three. Landlord/tenant struggles in Ireland and the role of Irish migrant pioneers have also recurred in the cinema. In isolating out primarily male screen professions in American cinema in chapter four, the Irish male is seen to have been sublimated into a very limited number of roles. By contrast, the representation of Irish women at work and in the domestic sphere, chapter five, is often far more complex.

THE RISING OF THE MOON (John Ford, Ireland, 1958, b&w)
John Ford shares poteen on set with Irish actors
Jack MacGowran (left), Cyril Cusack (seated) and Noel Purcell (standing).

Certain stars became associated with Irish-American roles: Colleen Moore, Pat O'Malley, Owen Moore, Charlie Murray, J Farrell MacDonald, James Cagney, Pat O'Brien, Spencer Tracy, Victor McLaglen, John Wayne and Mary Gordon. None of these was born in Ireland, but many actors came from Irish backgrounds. Cagney's father, for example, was an Irish saloon-keeper. Irish-American film directors included John Ford, Raoul Walsh and John Huston. While Ford is the most 'Irish' of American directors, the ethnic resonances which are carried in their films by other directors are sometimes so private that often only those viewers with an Irish background will recognise the trace. One of the reasons for this was that a feature of the establishment of the classical Hollywood cinema was to squeeze out the ethnically distinct elements of early cinema. By the 1930s, in a film such as THE PUBLIC ENEMY, the Irish milieu is only coded at the level of accent, gesture, context. Thus, this film about real Irish gangsters has no overt reference to Irishness in it. In the main, Hollywood continues in this way. What follows, therefore, is the tracing of these often indistinct lines from the early cinema to the present.

A different set of issues faces the Irish within European national cinemas where the emphasis is on Ireland's relationship to Britain. British cinema itself has presented a dark and brooding image of Irish politics and history, with the focus on the Irish as gripped by irrational, ahistorical forces. Furthermore, little context has been given in these films for the periodic eruptions of political violence. By contrast, American-based director Sidney Olcott, who made films in Kerry during 1910-14, clearly sided with Irish rebels in a cycle of historical dramas set during the 1798-1803 period.

Beyond the maelstrom of Irish history and politics is the placidity of the west of Ireland. Here, a continuing cycle of mainly foreign film-makers have chosen to present a bucolic Ireland free of work and care, with the Irish represented as consumers of drink and food, and only the occasional enjoyable fight to break the harmony. Work and enterprise, as in THE QUIET MAN, are associated with negative, acquisitive traits. Simmering beneath these views of the Irish is a much crueller image of the country represented in the work of Irish film-makers since the 1970s. Bob Quinn, Joe Comerford, Cathal Black and others have shown a bleaker and more violent vision of rural Ireland and its people. These film-makers and others, including Pat Murphy, Margo Harkin, Tommy McArdle, Kieran Hickey and Thaddeus O'Sullivan, have put on screen marginal groups in Irish society, as well as working class and middle class experience, previously unexplored versions of Irish history and politics, and the diverse traditions in Northern Ireland. This cycle of films laid the foundations for an Irish cinema in the 1970s and 1980s. Irish film-makers have since gone on to produce the more polished, but perhaps less challenging, Irish cinema of the 1990s.

There is, of course, a small group of Irish film-makers, especially Neil Jordan, Jim Sheridan and Pat O'Connor, who are known worldwide and who have made most of their films with the support of British and American production companies. As with all European film-makers working for a mass commercial cinema audience, the local cultural bonds are loosened to encourage mainstream commercial distributors to show the films widely. The difficulty with this strategy is that the cinema images of Ireland produced may reinforce rather than challenge the perceived limitations of the Irish in the cinema. Nevertheless, these film-makers have helped open up spaces in the international film industry denied to previous generations. It is likely that many more younger Irish film-makers will follow their path.

What is collected here is a selection of frozen moments from across the decades of cinema and from around the world. As a record, it reminds us that the thousands of films that have been made (and lost) about the Irish constitute an important cultural legacy which the Irish Film Archive is committed to collecting and preserving.

Kevin Rockett.

GIU' LA TESTA

(A Fistful of Dynamite; Sergio Leone,
Italy, 1971, colour)

*During the Mexican Revolution, ex-IRA man
Sean Mallory, played by James Coburn,
recalls the act of betrayal to the authorities
in Ireland which led to his exile.*

Between 1916 and 1920, Ireland's first major film production unit, the Film Company of Ireland, made about twenty fiction films. One of its feature films was an adaptation of Charles Kickham's novel *Knocknagow* (Fred O'Donovan, 1918), and its final project was an adaptation of William Carleton's novel, *Willy Reilly and his Colleen Bawn*, which is set in the 18th century. While the centenary of the 1798 Rebellion came too early for fiction film-making to commemorate the anniversary, within fifteen years of the beginnings of the cinema, the attempts by Irish republicans during the 1798-1803 period to establish an independent Irish state became a popular subject for American film-makers. At least eleven films were made about these Irish rebellions in the five years before the 1916 Rising. The American company, Kalem, whose principal director, Irish-Canadian Sidney Olcott, is credited with making the first fiction film in Ireland, THE LAD FROM OLD IRELAND (1910), also made a number of historical dramas in the country.

From the 1920s to the 1950s Irish and non-Irish film-makers made feature films about the War of Independence. Though the charismatic Irish leader Michael Collins makes his first named cinema appearance in Neil Jordan's 1996 film, he had already appeared incognito as a character in four previous films: as 'The General' in THE KEY (Michael Curtiz, USA, 1934) and SHAKE HANDS WITH THE DEVIL (1959), as 'Commandant Carberry' in THIS OTHER EDEN (Muriel Box, Ireland, 1959), and as 'Dennis Riordan' in BELOVED ENEMY (1936). After World War Two, British film-makers brought to the screen the IRA's post-independence upsurge in political violence. Later, Irish, British and American film-makers explored the post-1969 phase of 'The Troubles'.

While concentrating on the exciting narrative possibilities of the republican struggle, the more mundane effects of partition on the south have been largely ignored by film-makers until recently. One of Sean O'Casey's anti-war plays, the Civil War drama *Juno and the Paycock*, was adapted by Alfred Hitchcock as an early British sound film, though the director readily acknowledged its limitations as cinema. It is indicative of the sensitivity to the memories of this period that only in the 1990s has the subject been visited by Irish film-makers and even then only within the context of narratives which examine the continuing tension and bitterness which sours rural communities in the 1950s.

WILLY REILLY AND HIS COLLEEN BAWN

(John MacDonagh, Ireland, 1920, b&w)

Set in the 1740s and 1750s, a Catholic gentleman, Willy Reilly (played by Brian Magowan, right), and a Protestant squire's daughter, Helen, the Colleen Bawn, (Frances Alexander, centre), fall in love. Another suitor is the bigoted Protestant, Whitecraft, (Jim Plant, left), who seeks to invoke the anti-Catholic Penal Laws in order to dispossess Willy of his family's ancestral lands and to end his relationship with Helen. With the aid of liberal Protestants, Whitecraft's bigotry is overcome, and Willy and Helen are eventually married, despite the reluctance of the Squire, (George Nesbit, back to camera), to sanction the union. By the 1790s, such peaceful resolution of conflict had evaporated as

a new generation of republicans fought in the 1798 Rebellion for an independent republic. This rebellion and the 1803 Rising were popular subjects for film-makers in the early 1910s. One of the earliest such films is RORY O'MORE, in which Kathleen, played by Gene Gauntier, the Kalem Company's top actress and scriptwriter, misleads English troops while her boyfriend, Rory (Sidney Olcott), a rebel, hides beneath her cloak. Later, Rory is captured and sentenced to death, but he escapes from the gallows with the aid of a priest and sails to America with Kathleen.

BOLD EMMETT, IRELAND'S MARTYR

(Sidney Olcott, USA, 1915, b&w)

The leader of the 1803 Rebellion, Robert Emmet, was a popular subject of plays and songs throughout the 19th century. He also received screen treatment from Sidney Olcott in one of the last films he made in Ireland, even if his version of the story (including the spelling of Emmet's name in the film's title) takes extended liberties with the historical facts. In BOLD EMMETT, IRELAND'S MARTYR the informer, (Robert Rivers or Robert Vignola, above with beard), gives evidence during Emmet's (Jack Melville, in dock) trial for treason, while Olcott himself can be seen as a member of the

courtroom crowd. One of the recurring representations of the Irish in the cinema is the informer, whose images - black cloaked, slinking, deformed or dim-witted - is a representation of the failure of the Irish through internal division to overcome the British presence in Ireland. In most instances the informer is killed, as in the two adaptations of Liam O'Flaherty's novel (see over). In ANNE DEVLIN, the real historical person, Anne Devlin (Bríd Brennan), resists the pressures of British military officer Major Sirr (Ian McElhinney) during her imprisonment after the 1803 Rebellion.

THE INFORMER

(Arthur Robison, GB, 1929, b&w)

Lars Hanson (right) as informer Gypo Nolan.

Victor McLaglen (right) as Gypo Nolan, a performance for which he won an Oscar.

MY WILD IRISH ROSE

(David Smith, USA, 1922, b&w)

Dion Boucicault was one of the most popular Irish playwrights of the 19th century. Amongst the many adaptations of his plays is MY WILD IRISH ROSE, which is derived from *The Shaughraun* (1874). During the Fenian agitation of the 1860s, magistrate Corry Kinchela (James Farley, left), and an informer conspire to deprive Robert Ffolliott, (Edward Cecil, right), of his property by framing him on a Fenian conspiracy charge. With the help of Conn, the Shaughraun, Robert escapes from the ship transporting him to Australia and subsequently overcomes Kinchela's malevolence.

The constitutional Irish campaigns at Westminster during this period never recovered from the box-office trouncing

of PARNELL. In this film, a benevolent Charles Stewart Parnell, (played by beardless Clark Gable), helps the Irish

tenant farmers during the Land War, but his Home Rule crusade is reduced to ruin because of his relationship with

Mrs O'Shea, (Myrna Loy).

THE PLOUGH AND THE STARS

(John Ford, USA, 1936, b&w)

The defining moment for Irish separatists was the 1916 Rising. Due to the high cost of recreating period detail and battle scenes, one of the few films which seeks to portray these events is this adaptation of Sean O'Casey's anti-war play, *The Plough and the Stars*. In John Ford's Hollywood-produced version of the play, the drama is largely confined to Nora Clitheroe's (Barbara Stanwyck) concern for the preservation of her domestic sphere and the well-being of her husband, Jack Clitheroe (Preston Foster), a commander in the Irish Citizen Army.

As Irish nationalists fought for an independent island-nation, Ulster unionists sought to preserve their constitutional links with the British Crown. Northern Ireland's Protestant and unionist cultures have been poorly served by the cinema. ASCENDANCY is one of the few films made about this tradition, but, here, as elsewhere, unionists are often reduced to familiar stereotypes: bowler-hatted, sash-wearing marchers asserting their loyalty to the Crown through the memory of the sacrifice of the Somme, their military victory at the Boyne, or manipulating sectarian differences to ensure their economic and political dominance of a loyalist state.

IRISH DESTINY

(George Dewhurst, Ireland, 1926, b&w)

The War of Independence of 1919-21 provided the exciting action required by narrative cinema and a ready-made situation in which to centralise the hero and to include a romantic sub-plot. In IRISH DESTINY, the first fiction film made about the war, Paddy Dunne Cullinan plays an IRA man, Denis O'Hara, who is seen above as he approaches an IRA meeting place to be inducted into the organisation.

Made by film production novices in the Killarney area, THE DAWN was billed as the authentic voice of Irish cinema and retains its status today as the most significant indigenous Irish feature film of the early sound era. Utilising local talent (including many who had participated in the real War of Independence fifteen years earlier) and minimal resources, the heroic conditions of production have often obscured what is in effect a conventional drama about the IRA fighting against the Black and Tans and how a family overcomes the taint of informer. In the scene above, Tom Cooper, the film's director and leading actor as the local IRA leader, uses modern communications to plan an ambush against the Tans.

SHAKE HANDS WITH THE DEVIL

(Michael Anderson, GB/USA, 1959, b&w)

During the War of Independence, the IRA, led by Sean Lenihan (James Cagney, centre), and with Kerry O'Shea (Don Murray, left, in British uniform), an Irish-American who joins the IRA after a friend is killed by the British, Terence O'Brien (Richard Harris, second from right) and Chris Noonan (Cyril Cusack, right), kidnap Jennifer Curtis (Dana Wynter), the daughter of a British official, as a hostage for an imprisoned IRA member. Unlike his colleagues, Lenihan refuses to accept the Truce which leads to the 1921 Anglo-Irish Treaty, and, intent on continuing the war, plans to kill the hostage. As he is about to

execute her, O'Shea shoots him and then throws away his gun, symbolising the end of the war. In BELOVED ENEMY, the charismatic IRA leader, Dennis Reardon (Brian Aherne), is encouraged during the Treaty negotiations by Lady Helen (Merle Oberon), daughter of Lord Athleigh (Henry Stephenson, right), a British diplomat, to forsake the gun for peace. While Reardon's role was based on the real-life Michael Collins, Lady Helen's is a barely disguised version of Collins' mythical relationship with Lady Lavery.

BELOVED ENEMY

(H C Potter, USA, 1936, b&w)

On his return to Ireland after signing the Anglo-Irish Treaty, Dennis Reardon (Brian Aherne) is shot by one of his former colleagues as he pleads for peace. Unfortunately, the death of Reardon/Collins was the sort of downbeat ending so disliked by Hollywood in its classical period. To overcome this problem, the producers made two endings

so that film exhibitors could choose whether to have Reardon die, or

to be re-united with his sweetheart, Lady Helen (Merle Oberon), whom

he tells he will not die. In the first feature film with Michael Collins as

a named character, Liam Neeson plays the Irish leader.

OURSELVES ALONE
(Brian Desmond Hurst, GB, 1936, b&w)

British Cinema only rarely touched on the reasons for the War of Independence. In fact, the Chief Censor at the British Board of Film Censors during the 1920s and 1930s, Colonel Hanna, who had served as a British military officer in Ireland during the war, discouraged film-makers from exploring the period. Hanna was also probably involved in the banning of IRISH DESTINY in 1926. Unlike their American and Irish counterparts, British films dealing with Irish history and politics tended to represent violence, as is common in British cinema in general, as debilitating and negative, destroying both the family and personal relationships. One of the few ways British cinema imagined overcoming this cycle of violence in Ireland was when the heroine became romantically

involved with a British officer. In the case of the War of Independence film OURSELVES ALONE, Maureen Elliott (Antoinette Cellier), the sister of an IRA leader, Terence (Niall McGinnis, right), is in love with a British officer, Wiltshire (John Loder), who kills her brother. Another suitor is an Irish police officer, Hannay (John Lodge, left), who takes the blame for the death knowing that Maureen really loves Wiltshire. In I SEE A DARK STRANGER, Bridie Quilty (Deborah Kerr), manages to overcome her hatred of the British, especially the ingrained memory of Oliver Cromwell, and her pro-Nazi sympathies during World War Two to help her new-found boyfriend, a British officer, to keep secret the Allied plans for the invasion of Europe.

ODD MAN OUT

(Carol Reed, GB, 1947, b&w)

The political partition of Ireland in 1920, and the subsequent periodic eruptions of political violence by Irish republicans seeking to establish an island-nation, continue to feature in British cinema. Within the British narrative tradition, the single, usually irreversible, act of violence at the beginning of the film seals the fate of the character, as with Johnny (James Mason) in ODD MAN OUT, where a robbery by the IRA in Belfast goes badly wrong and a guard is killed. Despite the efforts of his girlfriend, Kathleen (Kathleen Ryan), the doom-laden

trajectory of the film ensures that the politics of the British presence in Ireland will not be explored. Joe Comerford's indigenous Irish feature, HIGH BOOT BENNY, on the other hand, seeks to find a new visual language to explore the complexities of the post-1969 phase of republican rebellion in Northern Ireland and its effect on the South. In this scene, Benny (Marc O'Shea) has been tarred and feathered by the IRA as he crosses paths with the British army, loyalists and other terrorists.

THE GENTLE GUNMAN

(Basil Dearden, GB, 1952, b&w)

The voice of Irish mothers and grandmothers who have lost sons or husbands fighting the British presence in Ireland, such as Molly Fagan (Barbara Mullen) in THE GENTLE GUNMAN, is frequently raised against political violence. There is an opposing representation of Irish women which is of those who wish to encourage the men towards further sacrifice for 'The Cause'. The original cinematic version of this representation may be Maureen Fagan (Elizabeth Sellars), Molly's

daughter, in THE GENTLE GUNMAN. Maureen tries to convince her estranged boyfriend, reluctant IRA member Terence Sullivan (John Mills), to emulate the example of his brother Matt (Dirk Bogarde) in the IRA campaign during World War Two. This representation would also encompass such roles as Siobhan Donovan (Alison Doody) in A PRAYER FOR THE DYING (Mike Hodges, GB, 1987) and Jude (Miranda Richardson) in THE CRYING GAME.

A TERRIBLE BEAUTY

(Tay Garnett, GB, 1960, b&w)

The theme of reluctant IRA fighters who want to leave the organisation, such as Terence (John Mills) in THE GENTLE GUNMAN and Dermot O'Neill (Robert Mitchum, left, with fellow IRA member, Sean Reilly, played by Richard Harris, right) in A TERRIBLE BEAUTY, recurs in the various representations of the IRA. Having shown his mettle as an IRA man, Dermot wants to develop a relationship with Neeve Donnelly (Anne Heywood, centre), and when that doesn't prove possible in Ireland they migrate to England. The possibility of redemption through renunciation and love evidenced by Dermot in A TERRIBLE BEAUTY becomes impossible for subsequent characters such as Martin Fallon

(Mickey Rourke) in A PRAYER FOR THE DYING and Fergus (Stephen Rea)

in THE CRYING GAME, in that the IRA follow them to England to exact

retribution for their desertion of the organisation. Another migrant is

ex-IRA man Seamus Flaherty (Sterling Hayden, right) who had fought in

the War of Independence before going to America, but whose grandson,

Michael (John Paul Leeming), in THE OUTSIDER is mesmerised by his

tales of the age-old struggle against the English. When Michael becomes

an adult he goes to Ireland to join the IRA, but he finds that both that

organisation and the British want to use him for propaganda purposes.

BROKEN HARVEST

(Maurice O'Callaghan, Ireland, 1994, colour/b&w)

In BROKEN HARVEST, Arthur O'Leary (Colin Lane, right), who had fought on the anti-Treaty side in the Civil War, has an on-going feud with Josie McCarthy (Niall O'Brien, left). Arthur's son tries to come to terms with the intensity of the struggle between the two men as he recalls his childhood in 1950's Ireland from the vantage point of 1980's New York.

John Doyle (Donal Donnelly, left) not only fought on the anti-Treaty side but witnessed from his prison cell the execution of a republican. In these films, those on the anti-Treaty side are perceived as having suffered economic disadvantage as a result of their stance. John Doyle, for example, loses his established fishing rights in the face of modernisation and plans for the anticipated influx of tourists which is being aided by his Civil War enemy, Ben Moran (Vass Anderson, right).

RIO GRANDE

(John Ford, USA, 1950, b&w)

In the last of John Ford's Cavalry trilogy, Kathleen Yorke, played by Maureen O'Hara, visits the west where her husband (John Wayne) and son are soldiers. One of the film's most moving scenes occurs shortly after her arrival, when Kathleen is serenaded in the company of her estranged husband by the Irish love song, "I'll Take You Home Again, Kathleen".

Migration was one of the most painful events for Irish communities. Until well into the 20th century, most of those who left Ireland for the USA or Australia never returned home, or if they did, it was likely to be for a single visit in their lifetimes. Thus, the 'American Wake' was a form of burial of memory, though the financial remittances from relatives abroad were an important source of income for many Irish families. It is not surprising, therefore, that in Sidney Olcott's THE LAD FROM OLD IRELAND (USA, 1910), the migrant who has made good in New York returns home with his newly-acquired wealth just in time to save his girlfriend and his mother from eviction. Most migrants, though, did not return to Ireland, and it is the experience of the Irish in America which forms the bulk of the films made about the Irish abroad.

In the early decades of American cinema, many films were based on the interaction of ethnic groups. Of all the inter-ethnic films, Irish-Jewish stories were most frequently produced. Even before the huge success of the 1924 play *Abie's Irish Rose*, Irish-Jewish films were being made regularly. Not only did the Irish and Jewish populations in the USA amount to perhaps as many as ten million people who might frequent the cinema, but in an era when reformism sought to integrate America's diverse cultures into an American 'nation', the widely different religious, linguistic and cultural traditions of the Irish and the Jews were worth exploring. The integrationist ideology was sensibly promoted indirectly through humour, an established tradition in both Jewish and Irish cultures. The films had a consistent narrative line: feuding immigrant parents are forced to confront their prejudices when their American-born off-spring fall in love with someone from the other tradition. With Irish women integrating into American society more rapidly than men because of their higher earnings, films which explored inter-class relationships, especially of working class Irish women and upper class Anglo-Saxon men, were also frequently produced.

MOTHER MACHREE

(John Ford, USA, 1928, b&w)

Ellen McHugh (Belle Bennett) leaves Ireland with her son following the death of her fisherman husband in a storm. Meeting up with The Giant of Kilkenny (Victor McLaglen), she works in an American side-show and later as a housekeeper, an occupation in which many Irish women were employed in America. Ellis Island was literally the gateway to America. Its gauntlet of immigration officers

and medical staff had to be negotiated before entry was allowed to the USA. In GATEWAY, Dubliner Catherine O'Shea (Arleen Whelan) is more hindered than helped by fellow passenger, American war correspondent Dick Court (Don Ameche), as she finds herself confronting immigration officials on Ellis Island.

UP IN CENTRAL PARK

(William A Seiter, USA, 1948, b&w)

The multi-ethnic arrival outside the immigration centre in New York was a defining moment in the migrants new lives. UP IN CENTRAL PARK is a turn-of-the-century migration musical in which newly-arrived Irish migrants, Rosie Moore (Deanna Durbin), and her father, Timothy Moore (Albert Sharpe), centre above, help a crusading New York Times reporter with his campaign against political corruption in Tammany Hall. In FAR AND AWAY, Joseph Donnelly (Tom Cruise) and Shannon Christie (Nicole Kidman), who are from opposite ends of the Irish social spectrum, arrive in Boston.

DINTY

(Marshall Neilan, USA, 1920, b&w)

After Doreen O'Sullivan (Colleen Moore) arrives with her son Dinty in San Francisco from Ireland, she finds out that her husband died that day. When his mother also dies after working hard as a scrub woman, twelve year-old Dinty (Wesley Barry, standing) fends for himself and helps the police smash a Chinese opium smuggling ring. Here, Dinty is the 'conductor' of a multi-ethnic orchestra. In the comedy, HIS FAMILY TREE, Patrick Murphy (James Barton, centre), who has just arrived in the USA, is bemused as his son's political henchmen,

campaign manager Stonehill (Herman Bing, left) and publicist Mike Donovan (Addison Randall, right), want to hide him. But then, his son who is running for office, has changed his name to 'Murfree' as a means of making himself appear more acceptable to some voters. This denial of ethnic background causes the loss of the Irish vote, a constituency only restored to him when the Murfrees acknowledge their Irish origins.

THE GUTTERSNIPE

(Dallas M Fitzgerald, USA, 1922, b&w)

Shopgirl Maisie O'Day (Gladys Walton) from New York City's Little Ireland lives her life through the fantasies she reads in magazines. She mistakes soda counter clerk Dennis O'Day (Walter Perry) for an English nobleman she has been reading about, and though he turns out to be masquerading in a dress suit, he still becomes her boyfriend. When Dennis is arrested on a counterfeiting charge, Maisie finds advice in a magazine which succeeds in capturing

the real counterfeiters. The young couple receive a reward which they use to leave Little Ireland. BRINGING UP FATHER is one of many filmed versions of George McManus' hugely popular 'Jiggs and Maggie' newspaper cartoon. In this film, down-to-earth Jiggs (J Farrell MacDonald), and his socially-ambitious wife, Maggie (Polly Moran), enjoy a laugh at Dinty Moore's pub as the customers forsake the drink for a brawl.

ABIE'S IRISH ROSE

(Victor Fleming, USA, 1929, b&w)

In ABIE'S IRISH ROSE, Abie Levy (Charles Rogers, centre) meets Rosemary Murphy (Nancy Carroll, centre) while they are in France during World War One. On their return to the USA, they are married in an Episcopal church. Concerned at his father's response to her Irish-Catholic background, Abie gets Rosemary to tell him that her name is Rosie Murpheski. Mr Levy insists that a rabbi marry them again. Just after the wedding ceremony, Rosemary's father (J Farrell MacDonald, left) arrives with a Catholic priest, Father Whalen (Nick Cogley, in picture), and insists on a Catholic ceremony. By then the young couple have become alienated from both parents, but when twins are born the generations are reunited.

The Irish-Jewish seven-film series 'The Cohens and the Kellys' was made between 1926 and 1933 and was similar in structure to ABIE'S IRISH ROSE. Throughout the comedy series, feuding parents reluctantly come to terms with their children's relationships. Though George Sidney played the part of 'Jacob Cohen' in all seven films, 'Patrick Kelly' was played in one film each by J Farrell MacDonald and Mack Swain, actors who, like Murray, played many 'Irish' roles.

l to r Vera Gordon (Mrs Cohen), George Sidney (Jacob Cohen), Olive Hasbrouck (Nannie Cohen), Charlie Murray (Patrick Kelly), Jason Robards (Tim Kelly), Kate Price (Mrs Kelly).

PAGAN LOVE

(Hugo Ballin, USA, 1920, b&w)

One of the most extreme Irish representations of inter-racial relationships is found in PAGAN LOVE. In this film, which was influenced by D W Griffith's BROKEN BLOSSOMS (1919), a young, but blind, woman from an Irish-Jewish family, Kathleen Levinsky (Mabel Ballin), is befriended by a young Chinese man, Tsing Yu-Ch'ing (Togo Yamamoto). When a college friend of Tsing's, Dr Hardwick, meets Kathleen he offers to operate on her eyes. Her sight restored, Kathleen flees in fear from Tsing when she sees that he is oriental. Wounded in love, Tsing returns to China and commits suicide, while Kathleen and Dr Hardwick develop their relationship.

John Ford was already well versed in the 1920s in contrasting the easy-going virtues of the Irish with other ethnic groups. While Ford's satire is at its most biting when he makes comparisons between the Irish and those with WASP backgrounds, (for example, Colonel Thursby played by Henry Fonda in FORT APACHE, 1948), Ford also satirised other ethnic groups. In RILEY THE COP, Irish policeman James Riley (J Farrell MacDonald, right), who has been a cop for twenty years without making an arrest, is contrasted with Eitel Krausmeyer (Harry Schultz), a German who is 'more military' in his job. When Riley is sent to Germany to bring back a suspect, he meets and falls in love with Krausmeyer's sister without knowing she is related to the policeman.

SATURDAY NIGHT

(Cecil B DeMille, USA, 1922, b&w)

The most painful cinematic transformations are often those in which Irish characters wish to move from their Irish-Catholic working class backgrounds to become part of the Anglo-Saxon Protestant upper class world. In SATURDAY NIGHT, Shamrock O'Day (Edith Roberts, above right), who like her mother (Sylvia Ashton, left), is a laundress, and is the girlfriend of Tom McGuire (Jack Mower, opposite), chauffeur for Iris Van Suydam (Leatrice Joy, opposite right). In the meantime, Iris's fiancé Richard becomes attracted to Shamrock, while Iris and

Tom also become lovers. As a result, Richard and Iris's engagement is called off, but the new partnerships don't work out as neither Shamrock nor Tom can adjust to their new surroundings. One night, Tom and Shamrock sneak off to Coney Island, and on their return find Iris and Richard waiting for them. Realising the errors they have all made, divorces are obtained, and Tom marries Shamrock, while Richard weds Iris.

IRENE

(Alfred E Green, USA, 1926, b&w/colour)

Irene O'Dare (Colleen Moore) leaves her Philadelphia Irish working-class environment and goes to New York where she meets upper class Donald Marshall (Lloyd Hughes). He helps her train as a model and they fall in love, though his snobbish mother engages a genealogist to investigate Irene's family roots. To Mrs Marshall's horror and Irene's embarrassment, her washerwoman mother appears during a fashion show. Irene runs home, but she is followed

by Donald who declares his love for her, despite his mother's objections to her background. This film was a huge hit and helped propel 'flapper girl' Colleen Moore to stardom. A 1940 remake by Irish-born Herbert Wilcox was less successful. In that film, Anna Neagle played Irene, Ray Milland (right) is Donald Marshall, and Alan Marshal plays Donald's friend Bob Vincent, who invests in the dress shop where Irene works.

THE VALLEY OF DECISION

(Tay Garnett, USA, 1945, b&w)

In 1870s Pittsburgh Irish maid, Mary Rafferty (Greer Garson) and steel mill owner's son Paul Scott (Gregory Peck) fall in love. The relationship appears doomed when her father Pat (Lionel Barrymore) is killed during a strike at the mill. Paul marries a childhood friend, but they are unhappy together. When Mrs Scott (Gladys Cooper) dies, Mary inherits her share in the mill and supports Paul against his wife in his desire to keep the mill open. Paul separates from her and is reunited with Mary. Irish-born actress Greer Garson won her fifth-in-a-row Oscar nomination as Best Actress for this film.

l to r Greer Garson, Dan Duryea, Gladys Cooper, Marshall Thompson, Marsha Hunt, Gregory Peck.

Kitty Foyle (Ginger Rogers, standing right) is from a Philadelphia Irish working class family and feels uncomfortable at the society home of her husband, Wyn Stafford (Dennis Morgan, right). At a family gathering, Kitty is instructed by Wyn's mother (Gladys Cooper, centre) in the ways of the family. Running from the oppressive environment, Kitty goes to New York and her marriage to Wyn is annulled. Years later, when Wyn wants to resume their relationship, Kitty chooses instead, a stable, if dull, life with a doctor.

DARK VICTORY

(Edmund Goulding, USA, 1939, b&w)

JESSICA'S GIRL

The social gulf dooms the possibility of a relationship between Irish
stable hand Michael O'Leary (Humphrey Bogart) and his boss,
society beauty Judith Traherne (Bette Davis).

Irish-American, and later Irish citizen, John Huston, has as his first screen heroine the cool Mary Astor with the ethnically distinct name of Brigid O'Shaughnessey playing an atypical 'Irish' role opposite Humphrey Bogart's Sam Spade.

A SON OF HIS FATHER

(Victor Fleming, USA, 1925, b&w)

Irish migrant Nora O'Shea, played by Bessie Love, travels to the American west where her brother works for a sheep rancher, Morgan. After helping capture a gang of smugglers, Nora marries Morgan.

Irish migrants settled mainly in the eastern American cities of New York, Boston, Philadelphia and Pittsburgh, though other cities, especially Chicago and San Francisco, were also the destinations of a great many Irish. In Australia, Sydney and Melbourne have been closely associated with the Irish. Less well known is the role of the Irish in helping colonise the pioneer territories of the American and Australian wildernesses, because the documentation, as much as the cultural interest, about the Irish in these areas seems to be lacking.

Most of the early Irish migrants to Australia went there involuntarily as transported convicts. Many were political prisoners who stayed in the Australian colonies after been freed from the prison camps. Others escaped from prison, as in THE PIONEERS (1916 and 1926), where Irishman Dan Farrel (Winter Hall, 1916; Augustus Neville, 1926) creates a new life for himself in the bush. Many of the films made in Australia about the Irish are based on real people, such as bushrangers. Most notable of these was Ned Kelly and his gang, the subject of many films, including the first Australian feature film, THE STORY OF THE KELLY GANG (1906).

In Ireland, the struggle for the land was also bound up with the assertion of sovereignty and the establishment of an independent state, though viewing the films on the subject one would not usually be led to that conclusion. Cinema has also tended to favour a pre-modern, pre-market view of the country. As a result, industrial modernisation and the integration of Ireland in the international market economy has not been of concern to film-makers. Rather, cinema tends to favour representations which seek to draw on notions of undifferentiated community and the uncritical assertion of 'Irish rural values'.

IN OLD CHICAGO

(Henry King, USA, 1938, b&w)

In the mid-West, Irish pioneer Michael O'Leary (J Anthony Hughes, centre), heads for Chicago where years later his wife Molly's (Alice Brady, right) heifer knocks over a lamp which allegedly causes the Chicago fire of 1871. In safety on Lake Michigan as the fire rages around them, Molly, her son Dion (Tyrone Power) and Dion's wife witness the city's destruction and re-affirm Michael's ambition to build a great city.

In the South, Gerald O'Hara (Thomas Mitchell, left) was an early Irish pioneer. Taking the name of his plantation and house from the Hill of Tara of his native County Meath in Margaret Mitchell's popular novel, he develops the property only to find himself on the losing side in the Civil War. While the war ravages the plantation, and the South is defeated militarily, his daughter Scarlett (Vivien Leigh, third from left), gains strength through the land to start restoring the plantation. After Rhett Butler walks out on her, she wonders, 'What is there that matters?' She hears her father's voice tell her that 'the land's the only thing that matters - it's the only thing that lasts.'

THE IRON HORSE

(John Ford, USA, 1924, b&w)

In the West, the completion of the transcontinental railway in 1869 at Promontory Point (above) was the symbolic moment in defining the American 'nation'. In John Ford's cinematic version of the project, three colourful Irish ex-soldiers: Sergeant Slattery (Francis Powers), Private Mackay (James Welch) and Corporal Pat Casey (J Farrell MacDonald, right), lead the multi-ethnic workforce with variations on the Irish-American work song, 'Drill, Ye Tarriers, Drill!'. In this instance at least, Ford's vision of the Irish is seeing them at the service of

WASP expansionism into the West as they help railroad entrepreneur Thomas Marsh (William Walling, left) complete the project. UNION PACIFIC, Cecil B DeMille's version of the same event, placed an Irish woman, postmistress Mollie Monahan (Barbara Stanwyck, centre), and her train-driving father (J M Kerrigan) at the centre of the action. While the crews meet once more at Promontory Point, the triangular relationship of Mollie and her lovers (Joel McCrea, Robert Preston) dominates the film.

FAR AND AWAY

(Ron Howard, USA, 1992, colour)

Most Irish migrant film stories end in east coast American cities, but an exception is FAR AND AWAY which moves its protagonists, Irish tenant farmer Joseph Donnelly (Tom Cruise, left) and his Anglo-Irish upper-class companion, Shannon Christie (Nicole Kidman), from rural Ireland to Boston in 1892 and then on to the 1893 Cherokee Strip land rush in Oklahoma. Before embarking on the last part of this land-grabbing journey, and re-unifying those differences apparently impossible within Ireland (landlord and tenant; Protestant and Catholic; male and female), Joseph confronts the Irish land agent Stephen (Thomas Gibson, right) who was directly responsible for his father's death and is Shannon's official beau.

The hard-working pioneer farmer is one aspect of the Irish representation in Australian cinema. The autobiographical account of the real-life O'Riordan family who carved a farm from the jungle in southeast Queensland was the subject of SONS OF MATTHEW. Central to the film is the rivalry between Shane O'Riordan (Michael Pate) and his brother Barney (Ken Wayne) for Cathie McAllister (Wendy Gibb), the daughter of a Scottish pioneer.

'YOU REMEMBER ELLEN'

(Sidney Olcott, USA, 1912, b&w)

In Ireland, the harsh life of a young peasant girl, Ellen (Gene Gauntier), is transformed when a young aristocrat, William (Jack Clark), disguised as a peasant, meets her and they fall in love and marry. They leave her area to seek their fortune elsewhere. Eventually they come to a mansion, and to her surprise, it transpires that he is Lord, and now she is Lady, of Rosna Hall. Such idealised transformations of their material lives was open to very few in the Irish countryside.

An old man, Marty (Jack Clark), tells how in the mid-19th century, a priest, Father Falvey (Sidney Olcott), got into trouble for supporting penniless tenants who are about to be evicted by their landlord. The White Boys, a secret agrarian society, of which Marty is a member, come to his aid, and after they deal with an informer, Michael Dee (Robert Vignola), the priest escapes to America. Peggy (Alice Hollister), Marty's girlfriend, is sentenced to seven years in jail for helping with the rescue. Now, fifty years later, Marty is married to Peggy and he announces that she too is there to tell the story.

KNOCKNAGOW

(Fred O'Donovan, Ireland, 1918, b&w)

In Charles Kickham's popular rural novel *Knocknagow*, which is set in Tipperary shortly after the Famine of the 1840s (though the film seems to be set in 1848), the land agent, Pender (J M Carre, right) threatens Mrs Honor Lahy (possibly Brenda Burke, left) and her daughter Norah (Kathleen Murphy, seated) with eviction unless they pay their rent arrears. Independent freeholder Mat the Thrasher (Brian Magowan,

second from right) challenges Pender's plan to clear the land of tillage farmers and change their holdings to more profitable grazing. With frequent evictions occurring during and after the Famine, tenant farmers organised to achieve ownership rights over the land. In PARNELL, Irish leader Charles Stewart Parnell (Clark Gable) surveys the aftermath of an eviction during the Land War of 1879-81.

CAPTAIN BOYCOTT

(Frank Launder, GB, 1947, b&w)

In CAPTAIN BOYCOTT, Parnell (Robert Donat) preaches the peaceful ostracism of the landlord, Captain Charles Boycott, whose name has ever since been associated with the concept of shunning a person in a community. By contrast, in the same film, the rabble-rousing

Hugh Davin (Stewart Granger) seeks to motivate a secret gathering of tenants to direct action against landlords, but when violence is unleashed by the community, it proves to be self-defeating and the calming rationalism of parliamentarianism is endorsed by the film.

THE QUIET MAN

(John Ford, USA, 1952, colour)

Industrialisation and modernisation of agricultural production has been generally eschewed by those seeking to promote an image of the country as pre-modern and hostile to mechanisation. In THE QUIET MAN, Red Will Danaher (Victor McLaglen, centre, with his sister Kate, played by Maureen O'Hara, and employee Feeney, played by Jack MacGowran) is an object of ridicule because he is a moderniser and has industrialised production on his farm. Changing the periodisation of John B Keane's play from the late 1950s/early 1960s, a time of great change in Irish society, to the 1930s allowed

THE FIELD to reinforce the pre-modern view of Ireland which has long been dominant in the cinema. In the film, Bull McCabe (Richard Harris) asserts a moral right to a field as he refuses to accept the notion that there can be a market in land. Even in the 1930s, the market was primary in cinema as much as in Irish agriculture, and the market continues to dictate that the version of rural Ireland which is seen on foreign cinema screens is one that has yet to enter the modern world.

HUNGRY HILL

(Brian Desmond Hurst, GB, 1947, b&w)

Few films set in the Irish countryside deal with industrialisation. Adapted from the novel by Daphne du Maurier, HUNGRY HILL is based on the real events in the copper-mining area of Berehaven, Allihies, County Cork in the 19th century when a family of Cornish miners developed a mine there. In the film, some locals object to the mine, then attack and destroy it. Afterwards, mine owner John Brodrick (Cecil Parker) laments the death of his son Henry (Michael Denison), who is killed in the explosion.

Two unemployed men, Vinnie Galvin (Stephen Brennan, left) and his brother-in-law Arthur (Eamon Morrissey), decide to build a Wall of Death in Vinnie's vegetable garden in the Bog of Allen. An innovative feature of the film is its location in the Irish midlands, where pioneering turf-cutting technology has been developed, but which is also a landscape that subverts the traditional cinematic expectations of Ireland as solely having the rugged mountains of the west.

THE PLAYBOYS

(Gillies MacKinnon, GB, 1992, colour)

Irish policeman Hegarty, played by Albert Finney, arrests travelling entertainer Tom (Aidan Quinn) less for a breach of the peace than because of Tom's relationship with Hegarty's ex-lover.

The most frequent representations of Irish men in American cinema have been in a small handful of action professions: firemen, policemen, soldiers, priests, politicians, gangsters, sportsmen and entertainers. These roles continue to be recycled in films such as BACKDRAFT (Ron Howard, USA, 1991) and FAR AND AWAY (1992). These professions reflected in the main the actual social reality of the Irish in America in earlier decades. With the Irish achieving important political leverage in the Democratic Party by the 1880s through their control of the all-important New York party headquarters at Tammany Hall, they gained direct access to municipal jobs, including policemen and firemen. Boxing, like crime, was one of the professions which allowed rapid social and financial advancement from poverty. Similarly, the 'Fighting Irish' was no myth, as the Irish were the largest ethnic group in the post-Civil War American army, itself a source of steady, if hard, employment.

The association of the Irish with the priesthood was also based on reality. Irish-American priests and bishops have been the most prominent ethnic group in the American Catholic Church for well over a century. Indeed, it was the Irish-American Catholic Hierarchy which pressurised Hollywood in the late 1920s and early 1930s to introduce a strict moral code on film production. The appearance of the Irish-American Catholic priest in the persons of Pat O'Brien, Spencer Tracy and Barry Fitzgerald was a direct response by Hollywood to such pressures. With a long Irish tradition in vaudeville variety theatre, it is not surprising to find many Irish characters in the musicals of the 1930s and 1940s. The image of the Irish entertainer is not generally seen against the backdrop of the Jazz Age, but rather against that of the late 19th century and within the context of the nostalgia for the pre-cinema's direct experience with the audience. The wider range of professions occupied by the Irish after World War Two are generally not represented in the cinema.

The strength of American genre cinema is such that its successful transfer to other cultures is rarely possible. At the purely urban visual level, Ireland is especially disadvantaged when tackling the conventions of the thriller genre. This is clear from the opening shots of THE COURIER (1988) where Dublin simply cannot compete with American cities in terms of visual impact. In the 1970s and 1980s, the American gangster was redefined by THE GODFATHER films and in the process positioned the Italian gangster at the centre of the genre, as was the case with LITTLE CAESAR (1931), which was released almost six months before THE PUBLIC ENEMY. GOODFELLAS (1990), STATE OF GRACE (1990) and MILLER'S CROSSING (1991) are unusual in recent decades in that they include Irish gangsters at the centre of the action.

GENTLEMAN JIM

(Raoul Walsh, USA, 1942, b&w)

John L Sullivan and 'Gentleman Jim' Corbett were two of the most prominent Irish-American boxers. Both had biographical feature films made about them. GENTLEMAN JIM starred Errol Flynn (above) in the title role, while Ward Bond played John L Sullivan.

Father Joe (Robert Edeson, centre) mediates between two rival Irish gang leaders, George D'Arcy (George O'Brien, left) and Big Tim Ryan (William Russell, right). His solution is to stage a boxing match between them at the parish house with himself the only spectator.

ONE-ROUND HOGAN

(Howard Bretherton, USA, 1927, b&w)

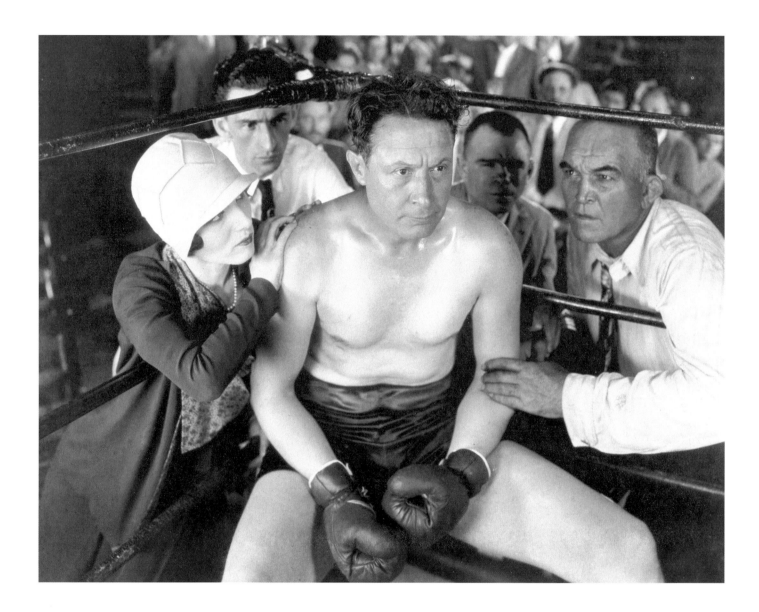

Robert Emmet Hogan (Monte Blue, centre), son of a former boxer, Tim Hogan, (who is played by the real-life ex-boxer James J Jeffries) is in love with Helen Davis (Leila Hyams) who abhors fighters and does not know that he is the light heavyweight champion of the world. After being wrongly accused of responsibility for the death in the ring of Helen's brother, Hogan fights to clear his name. Fighting without conviction, Hogan is being beaten because he is upset that Helen is annoyed with him for continuing to fight. Listening to the fight on the radio, Helen eventually relents and comes to the boxing arena.

Her presence motivates Hogan to beat his opponent, while he is also cleared of her brother's death. In KNOCKOUT REILLY Dundee Reilly (Richard Dix), a New Jersey steel mill worker, meets Mary Malone (Mary Brian), whose brother Pat is a defeated boxer. Reilly knocks out Killer Agerra when he tries to force himself on Mary, and then trains for a scheduled bout with Agerra. While in prison after being framed for a shooting, Reilly gets himself in shape for the fight. Acting on a hunch, Mary tells Reilly at the ringside that Agerra framed him, and he is spurred on to victory.

LAUGHING IRISH EYES

(Joseph Santley, USA, 1936, b&w)

Singer-turned-boxer Danno O'Keefe (Phil Regan, standing right) knocks down Irish champion Tiger O'Keefe (Warren Hymer, on ground), whose trainer Joe Cronin (John Sheehan, in window left), is trying to sell Tiger to Pat Kelly of New York's Irish-American Athletic Club, who is in Ireland looking for a new champion. Danno is signed up instead of Tiger, but he proves to be a reluctant fighter. After becoming champion, he forsakes the ring for a career as a singer in radio and marriage to Pat's daughter Peggy.

Perhaps the most famous of all Irish screen fights is in THE QUIET MAN. After killing a man in the ring, ex-boxer Sean Thornton (John Wayne, right) comes to Ireland in order to leave behind the 'lousy money' economy of America. Eventually, but reluctantly, he fights his brother-in-law, Red Will Danaher (Victor McLaglen), for his wife's dowry and for her public honour. Unlike the individualism associated with boxing and business, this 'donnybrook' is a communal event with pauses for drink, betting, encouragement from the large gathering, and even an ironic reference by Michaeleen Og Flynn (Barry Fitzgerald) to the Queensbury Rules. It is a celebration of community rather than a serious fight to the finish. Both men, after all, get drunk together afterwards.

THE BIG PARADE

(King Vidor, USA, 1925)

There was fighting of a more serious kind in the trenches of World War One, though the image sometimes promoted by the cinema gives the impression that the soldiers were on holiday in France. In THE BIG PARADE, Irish barman-turned-soldier Bull O'Hara (Tom O'Brien, second from right) is one of three soldiers vying for the attentions of Frenchwoman Melisande (Renée Adorée) before they are sent to the front. Bull and his colleague Slim (Karl Dane, left) are killed, while wealthy Jim Apperson (John Gilbert, second from left) goes home disabled, but later returns to Melisande in France.

Despite his bravado talk, Brooklyn-Irish soldier Jerry Plunkett (James Cagney, left) is a coward when faced with the possibility of death on the battlefield. It is only when Father Francis Duffy (Pat O'Brien, standing centre) demonstrates his own bravery that Plunkett sacrifices himself for the sake of the regiment. The 69th was the famous Irish regiment from the Civil War and Father Duffy was its chaplain during World War One. Another real character in the film is 'Wild Bill' Donovan (played in the film by Irish-born George Brent, himself an ex-IRA member), who later ran the Office of Strategic Services, the predecessor of the CIA, and had a career in Republican Party politics.

THE SULLIVANS

(Lloyd Bacon, USA, 1944, b&w)

The five real-life Irish-American Sullivan brothers (left to right, standing) are George (James Cardwell), Frank (John Campbell), Joe (George Offerman Jr), Matt (John Alvin) and Al (Edward Ryan) who join the Navy with Commander Robinson (Ward Bond, above right) during World War Two. All of them are killed when the ship on which they are all serving is sunk in the Pacific. In THE LONG GRAY LINE, young Irish migrant Marty Maher (Tyrone Power, second from left)

joins the military academy of West Point with Captain John Pershing (Milburn Stone, left) and becomes the academy's athletics trainer. When he reaches seventy the authorities want him to retire. Marty appeals to President Eisenhower and he is granted an interview with the President. He pleads his case through telling his life story and he is allowed to remain at West Point.

BIG BROTHER

(Allan Dwan, USA, 1923, b&w)

Irish criminals and gang leaders were represented on the screen well before James Cagney made such a dramatic impact with his performance as Irish gangster Tom Powers in THE PUBLIC ENEMY. In BIG BROTHER, Irish gang leader Jimmy Donovan (Tom Moore, centre), from New York's Lower East Side, who, unlike Powers, wants to go straight and is helped by Father Dan and his girlfriend Kitty Costello (Edith Roberts, right). Following his wrongful arrest on a

robbery charge, Jimmy escapes, captures the culprits, clears his name and is reunited with Kitty. In THE PUBLIC ENEMY, Tom Powers (James Cagney, left) and Matt Doyle (Edward Woods) fend off an ambush from rival gangsters in the film which made Cagney a star. The film was based in part on real-life Irish gangsters, the Bugs Moran gang from Chicago, which had largely been wiped out by Al Capone in the Saint Valentine's Day Massacre of 1929.

THE PUBLIC ENEMY

(William A Wellman, USA, 1931, b&w)

Enjoying the good life as wealthy gangsters, Powers (James Cagney)

and Doyle (Edward Woods) meet Gwen Allen (Jean Harlow).

Returning to his New York roots, gangster Rocky Sullivan (James Cagney)

meets up again with his childhood sweetheart Laury (Ann Sheridan).

THE COURIER

(Joe Lee, Frank Deasy, GB, 1988, colour)

THE COURIER was the first Irish urban gangster feature film. In this film, Gabriel Byrne plays Dublin drugs dealer Val who uses a legitimate courier service to transport his merchandise around the city. In MILLER'S CROSSING, Gabriel Byrne (standing) plays Irish gangster Tom Reagan, who works for Irish crime boss Leo (Albert Finney, seated) during Prohibition. Under threat from rivals, and entangled in a complex sexual triangle, the dark and sombre mood complements

what is perhaps Byrne's best screen performance so far. Gabriel Byrne is one of the few Irish actors to gain international star status; the others are Liam Neeson, Patrick Bergin and Pierce Brosnan, but Brenda Fricker, Donal Donnelly and many other Irish actors work regularly in film and television on both sides of the Atlantic, though in common with previous generations of Irish actors, such as Cyril Cusack, Barry Fitzgerald and Noel Purcell, they are not given star roles.

MURPHY'S I.O.U.

(Henry Lehrman, USA, 1913, b&w)

Though not directed by him, (and it may be another film from the MURPHY THE COP series), Mack Sennett's manic

irreverence for the police in his popular Keystone Kops series is clearly inscribed in this film and in which he himself

can be seen with a policeman's baton. One of Sennett's Keystone Kops films, THE RIOT (1913), climaxes in the Irish

community of Shackville with an Irish/Jewish riot which the incompetent Kops try to break up, but they only add to

the chaos. Despite his reported lack of enthusiasm for Ireland, Sennett regularly returned to Irish subjects, including

a migrant story, KITTY FROM KILLARNEY (1926). In William Wyler's realistic HAS ANYONE HERE SEEN KELLY? traffic

cop Pat Kelly (Tom Moore) marries immigrant Mitzi Lavelle (Bessie Love) when a jealous ex-boyfriend tries to have

her deported.

SIDE STREET

(Malcolm St Clair, USA, 1929, b&w)

The three O'Farrell brothers live in New York. Jimmy (Tom Moore, centre) is a cop, John (Matt Moore, left) is an ambulance surgeon, and unknown to his brothers, Dennis (Owen Moore, right) is a bootlegger. When members of Dennis's gang ambush Jimmy, Dennis takes the hail of bullets, and dies in his brother's arms after having redeemed himself. The Moore brothers were perhaps the best known Irish-American film acting family of the silent era.

Policeman's daughter Nellie Kelly (Judy Garland) prepares to go to a dance against the wishes of her cantankerous but work-shy Irish grandfather, Michael Noonan (Charles Winninger). Michael has maintained a life-long feud with his son-in-law, Nellie's father (George Murphy), because he married Michael's daughter and she died giving birth to Nellie. When Michael eventually gets a job as a hansom cab driver, the three generations are reconciled.

TOP O' THE MORNING

(David Miller, USA, 1949, b&w)

American insurance investigator Joe Mulqueen (Bing Crosby, left) comes up against the vagaries of the Irish police (Barry Fitzgerald, second from left; Hume Cronyn, third from left) when he arrives to investigate the disappearance of the Blarney Stone which is insured by his company. Crosby and Fitzgerald had already appeared together as Catholic priests in GOING MY WAY (USA, 1944),

performances for which both of them won Oscars. One of the few

forays by British film historian and documentary film-maker Paul Rotha

into fiction film production was NO RESTING PLACE, which concerns a

family of Irish travellers, the Kyles, one of whom is played by

Jack MacGowran (kneeling at front), who are being harassed by Irish

policeman Mannigan (Noel Purcell).

STATE OF GRACE

(Phil Joanou, USA, 1990, colour)

By the 1980s, ambiguity, deceit and ethnic betrayal even in close personal and family relationships was the norm in the cinema. Having been away for a number of years, Terry Noonan (Sean Penn, right) returns to New York's Hell's Kitchen, a traditional Irish quarter which has been redeveloped for 'yuppies'. He meets an old friend, Jackie Flannery (Gary Oldman, left), who is a member of his brother Frankie's criminal gang. The gang does not know that Terry is a policeman who has been sent to sabotage an alliance being negotiated between the Irish and an Italian gang. When Frankie kills Jackie to placate the Italians, Terry exacts revenge in a shoot-out in an Irish bar on Saint Patrick's Day.

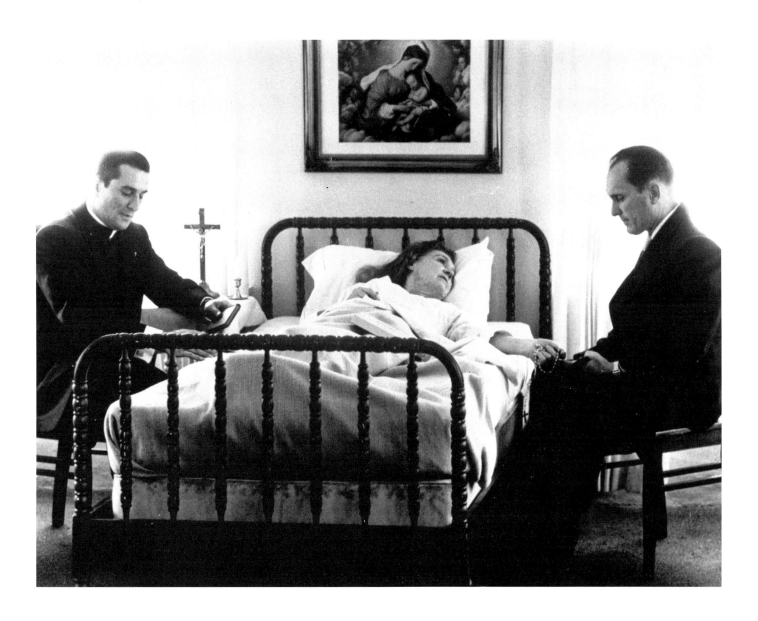

In TRUE CONFESSIONS, the corrupt underbelly of the Catholic Church meets an equally cynical police force in a narrative with film noir resonances. Irish policeman Tom Spellacy (Robert Duvall, right), who is working on a murder case, discovers that his brother Des (Robert De Niro, left), a powerful Catholic Church Monsignor, is a suspect in his enquiry. Despite the tension inherent in the investigation, a close bond continues to exist between the brothers, who visit their ill mother (Jeanette Nolan). Such a dark representation of the Catholic Church was a long way from the pristine cinematic image of the Irish-American Catholic priest in earlier decades.

ANGELS WITH DIRTY FACES

(Michael Curtiz, USA, 1938, b&w)

Catholic priest Father Jerry Connolly (Pat O'Brien, centre) convinces his childhood friend, defiant gangster Rocky Sullivan (James Cagney), to turn 'yellow' as he is about to be taken to the electric chair. Father Connolly wants Rocky to appear a coward so as to deflate his image in the eyes of the street kids (played by those who were shortly to be known as The Dead End Kids in a long series of films) who adore Rocky's bravura and cockiness. Pat O'Brien also played a priest in THE FIGHTING 69TH (1940) and in FIGHTING FATHER DUNNE

(1948), where he also sought to keep the Dead End Kids on the straight and narrow. Besides Pat O'Brien, Spencer Tracy is perhaps the best-known screen Catholic priest. As Father Tim Mullin in SAN FRANCISCO, he tries to protect Mary Blake (Jeanette MacDonald) from the attentions of Blackie Norton (Clark Gable, left). Tracy also played priests in BOYS TOWN (1938), where he was the real-life Father Edward Flannagan and for which he won an Oscar for Best Actor, and in its sequel MEN OF BOYS TOWN (1941).

THE SINGER NOT THE SONG

(Roy Baker, GB, 1961, colour)

In Mexico in the 1950s, Catholic priest Father Michael Keogh (John Mills in one of his many Irish roles) is trapped between male and female desire, between the attentions of the secret love of Locha (Mylène Demongeot) and of the church-hating Anacleto (Dirk Bogarde).

BLACK NARCISSUS

(Michael Powell, Emeric Pressburger, GB, 1947, colour)

In the Himalayas, a group of Catholic nuns set up a convent in the disused 'Palace of Women'. Their young superior is Sister Clodagh (Deborah Kerr, second from left) from Tipperary. Her memories of an unhappy love affair in Ireland are rekindled by the disturbing presence of Mr Dean (David Farrar) who lives nearby, and of the love affair between a local prince and a dancer. Unconsciously, they activate the suppressed sexual desires of the nuns, especially of Sister Ruth (Kathleen Byron, seated front), who provocatively discards her habit and taunts Clodagh with her reawakened sexuality. After Ruth dies while trying to push Clodagh over a precipice, Clodagh decides to abandon the convent.

In Ireland, control of education has been one of the preserves of the Catholic Church. Nuns, priests and religious brothers have been one of the main ways whereby the past, nationality and personal morality have been mediated for Irish children. In MAEVE, a complex debate between republicanism and feminism is also contextualised within a school where Margaret Lockhead plays a nun schoolteacher.

OUR BOYS

(Cathal Black, Ireland, 1982, b&w)

Sensitivity to the critique of the Catholic Church in Irish society is reflected in the fact that it was ten years before the indigenous film OUR BOYS was shown on Irish television. Using archival material, documentary interviews and dramatised sequences, it explores memories of the often harsh teaching regime of the Christian Brothers in Ireland. In this scene, Brother Kilmartin (Mick Lally) contemplates an uncertain future now that his superiors have sold the school in which he is teaching for a commercial redevelopment of the area.

An equally uncertain future faces a young priest (Donal McCann) in THE BISHOP'S STORY as he enjoys a pint in the local pub with his housekeeper and girlfriend (Maggie Fegan). Later, he tells his congregation at mass that shortly they will have another reason to call him father. His bishop doesn't take too kindly to his breaking of the celibate vows and before long his girlfriend has left the island and he is sent to the 'foreign missions' where he recalls his story in flashback to a fellow-exile, an alcoholic and paedophilic priest.

THREE CHEERS FOR THE IRISH

(Lloyd Bacon, USA, 1940, b&w)

Irish politicians are not well represented in the cinema. Certainly, John Ford's first non-western film as director, THE PRISONER OF AVENUE A (1920), featured an Irish political family, and one of Ford's key films about the Irish, THE LAST HURRAH, is centred on the political struggles between working-class Irish and WASP bankers in a barely-disguised Boston. In THREE CHEERS FOR THE IRISH, retired police officer Peter Casey (Thomas Mitchell, right) is annoyed when he is replaced in his job by a rookie cop, Scot Angus Ferguson (Dennis Morgan, left). Casey is also upset when his daughter, Maureen (Priscilla Lane, left), and Angus get married in secret because of Casey's opposition to the relationship. Despite the efforts of Maureen's sisters, Patricia (Virginia Gray, centre) and Heloise (Irene Hervey, right),

to effect a reconciliation, Casey remains hostile to Angus. Bored with retirement, Casey is encouraged by his daughters to stand for political office and is elected alderman. In THE LAST HURRAH Mayor Skeffington (Spencer Tracy, second from right) is surrounded by his life-long political lieutenants, Ditto Boland (Edward Brophy, standing), Sam Weinberg (Ricardo Cortez, left), Cuke Gillen (James Gleason, second from left) and John Gorman (Pat O'Brien, right) as he plans his last campaign. Skeffington's defeat signals the decline in Irish influence in big city 'machine politics', notwithstanding the election of Bostonian John F Kennedy as President two years after this film was released.

SWEET DADDIES

(Alfred Santell, USA, 1926, b&w)

Stage comedian Patrick O'Brien (Charlie Murray, right) prematurely celebrates his son's graduation from college and is fired from his act for being drunk. Patrick and Abie Finkleman (George Sidney) become business partners, but when they import molasses from the Bahamas, they are arrested as bootleggers. When the real bootlegger turns out to be the boyfriend of Abie's daughter, she and Patrick's son become engaged.

In contrast to his established gangster screen persona, in YANKEE DOODLE DANDY James Cagney sings and dances throughout this biographical film about Irish-American composer George M Cohan, whose patriotic song gives the film its title. Cagney, who was a vaudeville and Broadway stage performer before going to Hollywood in 1930, won an Oscar for his performance in this film.

GOODBYE BROADWAY

(Ray McCarey, USA, 1938, b&w)

Veteran vaudevillians Molly and Pat Molloy (Alice Brady, Charles Winninger) try to settle down when they buy a hotel,

but business life is not for them and they go back on the road.

Jimmy O'Dea, Ireland's most popular stage entertainer, appeared in a total of eleven films, including DARBY O'GILL AND THE LITTLE PEOPLE (USA, 1959) in which he played the king of the leprechauns. In LET'S BE FAMOUS, Jimmy Houlihan (Jimmy O'Dea) moves to London and meets with Betty Pinbright as they develop their singing careers.

THE MINSTREL BOY

(Sydney Morgan, GB, 1938, b&w)

Irish singer Mike (Fred Conyngham), leader of the popular band, the Minstrel Boys, meets Angela and marries her within twenty-four hours. Later, though, an ex-girlfriend, Dee Dawn, compromises him and threatens his marriage. Mike's performances deteriorate and his popularity wanes. He attempts suicide, but Angela arrives at his flat in time to save his life, and they begin life anew.

In this biographical film about composer Ernest R Ball (Dick Haymes, right), a medley of his songs, including 'A Little

Bit of Heaven (Shure They Call it Ireland)' and 'Mother Macree' concludes the film. The last song, 'When Irish Eyes

are Smiling', is performed by Ball and his girlfriend, Mary "Irish" O'Brien (June Haver).

INCENDIARY BLONDE

(George Marshall, USA, 1945, colour)

This film is about the life of Jazz Age singer and nightclub hostess, real-life Irish-American, Texas Guinan

(Betty Hutton), whose paternal grandparents had migrated from Ireland. In the film, her father Mike (Barry Fitzgerald)

joins in the mayhem from time to time as bootleggers and gangsters, boyfriends and nightclubs fall by the wayside.

Guinan was also a screen actress and appeared in more than thirty films between 1917 and 1933.

According to fellow musician Deirdre (Honor Heffernan), Danny (Stephen Rea) is 'the Stan Getz of South Armagh'.

LITTLE ANNIE ROONEY

(William Baudine, USA, 1925, b&w)

Only a small proportion of feature films have been produced by women. In this book, the films of only two Irish women directors, who have made a total of three feature films, are presented. In this chapter, which is primarily concerned with representations of women, only one woman film director, Margo Harkin, is included, though the work of director Pat Murphy, who is also very much concerned with representations of women, may be found elsewhere. This disproportionate number of female directors reflects the reality of film production. As a result, not only are most films produced by men, but in their films women are positioned in the domestic, rather than the public sphere, confirming a 'traditional' role for women and reinforcing the assertion of male power and authority within the family. For example, it is hard to imagine a cinematic reversal of genders in the shocking still, a publicity still we need to be reminded, from McFADDEN'S FLATS, which is reproduced here.

When women enter the male world of war and conflict, they are often represented as passive or neurotic bystanders of the action, as in LA JEUNE FOLLE and ASCENDANCY, and are usually acted upon rather than act independently. Occasionally, though, women have been represented as 'fiery' and capable of defining their own interests. Yet for all her struggle for independence, Mary Kate (Maureen O'Hara) in THE QUIET MAN only wants to be a housewife and to serve her husband. Representations of women as the waiting mother, wife or lover while the man participates in the male domain of acting on the world, recur in the cinema.

Family dramas, where the conflict between father and son is pronounced, have been a stable source for the cinema, but where women are usually the passive observers of this male struggle (STUDS LONIGAN; HOME IS THE HERO). The dysfunctional family is a major theme in Irish-American literature and has been the subject of filmed adaptations of some of its key plays, such as A LONG DAY'S JOURNEY INTO NIGHT (1960) and THE SUBJECT WAS ROSES (1968).

It was not until the 1960s, with the writings of Edna O'Brien and others, and their cinematic adaptations, O'Brien's GIRL WITH GREEN EYES (Desmond Davis, GB, 1964) and I WAS HAPPY HERE (1965), that the exploration of an independent sexual life for single and married Irish women was given popular expression. Central to these conflicts in Ireland, as in I CAN'T... I CAN'T..., was the still overbearing role of the Catholic Church and its prohibition on certain forms of contraception. With a new generation of Irish film-makers coming to the fore in the 1980s, the conflicts and dilemmas of young women were given more complete expression. For the first time, the drama of individual lives (TRAVELLER; MAEVE; HUSH-A-BYE BABY) was placed within the broader social and cultural contexts of Irish society.

THE CHURCH AND THE WOMAN

(Raymond Longford, Australia, 1917, b&w)

Irish-Australian Catholic Eileen Shannon (Lottie Lyell) and Dr Sidney Burton, a Protestant, want to marry, but Eileen's father is opposed to her marrying a non-Catholic. When Shannon is killed, Sydney is arrested, found guilty of his murder and sentenced to death. Meanwhile, Eileen brother, a Catholic priest, is told in confession by Mike Feeney (J P O'Neill, above) that he killed Shannon. Unable to get Feeney's permission to break the confidentiality of the confessional, Father Shannon claims that he killed his own father. Burton is freed, but by then the increasingly unstable Feeney has imprisoned Eileen. She escapes, Feeney is killed, and Eileen and Sydney can marry.

This is the first feature-length life of Patrick, the 5th century Welsh missionary who is believed to have defeated institutionalised paganism in Ireland and replaced it with christianity. Patrick and his sister Lupita (Alice Keating, above) are kidnapped in Wales by Irish raiders who bring them to Ireland where she is put on display at the slave market.

IRISH HEARTS

(Byron Haskin, USA, 1927, b&w)

The passive image of the Irish woman in Ireland and her transformation in America has been a recurring feature of the cinema. In IRISH HEARTS, Sheila (May McAvoy) follows her worthless boyfriend Emmett to America, but she becomes apprehensive en route when her father trades in her shamrock for a drink. In America, Emmett has taken up with Clarice, a flapper, and abandons Sheila. Meanwhile, Sheila meets a poor American

boy, Rory. On the day when Sheila is due to marry Emmett, he changes his mind and marries Clarice. Sheila appears at the wedding party, ascends the table, throws food and crockery at Emmett and the guests, and forces them into the street. Shortly afterwards, Rory finds the lost shamrock, and a contented Sheila agrees to marry him.

PEG O' MY HEART

(Robert Z Leonard, USA, 1933, b&w)

Taming the fiery Irish colleen through exposure to the English aristocracy was a central theme of J Hartley Manners hugely popular play *Peg o' My Heart* (1912), three versions of which were made for the cinema. The third of these adaptations has Marion Davies play Peg O'Connell who inherits two million pounds from her English relatives. A condition of the inheritance is that Peg has to live in England with the Chichesters. Reluctantly leaving her father, Pat

(J Farrell McDonald), she settles uneasily into the English environment, but she then falls in love with Sir Jerry Markham (Onslow Stevens), who has disguised his social status from her. She becomes outraged when she discovers that the Chichesters have been receiving £5,000 a year for keeping her and that Jerry has also been deceiving her. After returning to Ireland, Peg is celebrating with her father and friends when Jerry appears and asks her to marry him.

HELL CAT

(Reginald Barker, USA, 1918, b&w)

Irish women have only rarely been represented in the western but regardless of their nationality, women are most likely to be confined to domestic, saloon or educational settings. An exception is Pancha O'Brien (Geraldine Farrar), daughter of an Irish sheep ranch owner and a Spanish mother. She is in love with Sheriff Jack Webb and rejects the attentions of cattleman Jim Dyke who kills her father and kidnaps her. After appearing

to agree to marry Webb, Pancha kills him with a dagger and then accepts

Jack's marriage proposal. After 'stealing' a kiss from her in THE QUIET

MAN, Sean Thornton (John Wayne) is about to receive a slap from Mary

Kate Danaher (Maureen O'Hara) which quickly turns into a passionate

embrace.

LAUGHTER IN HELL

(Edward L Cahn, USA, 1933, b&w)

Central to American cinema's narrative development is the sexual triangle. In this film, Barney Stone (Pat O'Brien, right), an Irish mine worker in Tennessee, marries Marybelle Evans (Merna Kennedy), but returns home one day to find her making love to Grover Perkins (Arthur Vinton), a childhood adversary of Barney's. Enraged, Barney kills them both, gives himself up, and is sentenced to life imprisonment. Escaping from the prison camp, Barney meets up with Lorraine, whose parents have died in an epidemic, and they cross the state line to freedom.

Amongst the Brooklyn Irish at the turn of the century, Katie Nolan (Dorothy McGuire) tries to lift the family from poverty, but her husband Johnny (James Dunn, seated, who won an Oscar for Best Supporting Actor for his role) reverts to drunkenness and is frequently unemployed. Despite the attempts by a sympathetic policeman, Officer McShane (Lloyd Nolan), to help the family, Katie suppresses any other desire she may have for him.

THE COLLEEN BAWN

(Sidney Olcott, USA, 1911, b&w)

Dion Boucicault's *The Colleen Bawn* (1860) was one of the most popular Irish plays of the 19th century. The story of the secret 'marriage' by a defrocked priest of the beautiful peasant girl, Eily O'Connor, and her family's landlord, the impoverished Hardress Cregan, was adapted for the cinema many times during the early decades of the century. In 1911 alone, three filmed versions were made: one was produced in America, one in Australian, and this one in Ireland by the American company, Kalem. Despite the vicissitudes which befall her, including the attempted drowning by Danny Mann (Sidney Olcott), Cregan's half-witted employee, and her frosty

relationship with Cregan's mother (Agnes Mapes), who is unaware of her son's 'marriage', Eily awaits the public announcement of her marriage to Hardress. Mrs Cregan wants Hardress to marry the wealthy Anne Chute (Alice Hollister) in order to restore the family's declining fortunes. Though married, as she thinks, to Hardress Cregan (J P McGowan), Eily O'Connor (Gene Gauntier), continues her flirtatious relationship with her friend Myles na Coppaleen (Jack Clark, opposite). In THE LILY OF KILLARNEY, another adaptation of Boucicault's play, Eily O'Connor is played by Pamela Parr (centre), Barbara Gott is Sheelah and Henry Wilson is Danny Mann.

ASCENDANCY

(Edward Bennett, GB, 1983, colour)

The daughter of a prominent unionist employer, Connie (Julie Covington), is in psychological distress following the death of her brother during World War One, while the war on the home front also fuels her neurosis. In LA JEUNE FOLLE Catherine (Danièle Delorme, centre) is a strange young woman who lives in a convent and is haunted by

premonitions. She gets a feeling that her brother needs her, but, in fact,

he has been killed by the IRA as an informer. As she looks for her

brother, she is sheltered by the organisation and unknowningly falls in

love with her brother's murderer. When she discovers who killed her

brother, she seeks revenge and shoots him in a last embrace.

MY LEFT FOOT

(Jim Sheridan, Ireland, 1989, colour)

In this adaptation of Christy Brown's autobiographical novel, Christy (Hugh O'Conor) is dependent on his mother (Brenda Fricker) more than anyone else. Mrs Brown is a long-suffering mother who stoically accepts her responsibilities. Both Brenda Fricker and Daniel Day-Lewis, who played Christy as an adult, won Oscars for their performances, the first Irish-produced film to be so honoured.

In MAN OF ARAN, the burden of motherhood is embodied in Maggie
Dirrane carrying a back-breaking load of seaweed on the Aran Islands
as her husband, the Man of Aran, breaks stones to make a field.

THE PUBLIC ENEMY

(William A Wellman, USA, 1931, b&w)

While most people will remember Tom Powers (James Cagney) wisecracking cockiness and the gangster genre's gunfights as this film's central features, a major theme of the film is the tension within the family between bootlegger Tom and his law-abiding brother Mike (Donald Cook, right). Refusing to take sides between her sons is their mother (Beryl Mercer). In THE IRISH IN US, policeman Pat O'Hara

(Pat O'Brien, left) loses out to his boxing promoter brother Danny (James Cagney) over Olivia de Havilland, but it is their mother (Mary Gordon) who resolves the family feud. Unlike in THE PUBLIC ENEMY, where the delivery of Tom's dead body to their home is the consequence of his anti-social behaviour, in THE IRISH IN US family harmony is restored, albeit in the boxing ring.

McFADDEN'S FLATS

(Richard Wallace, USA, 1927, b&w)

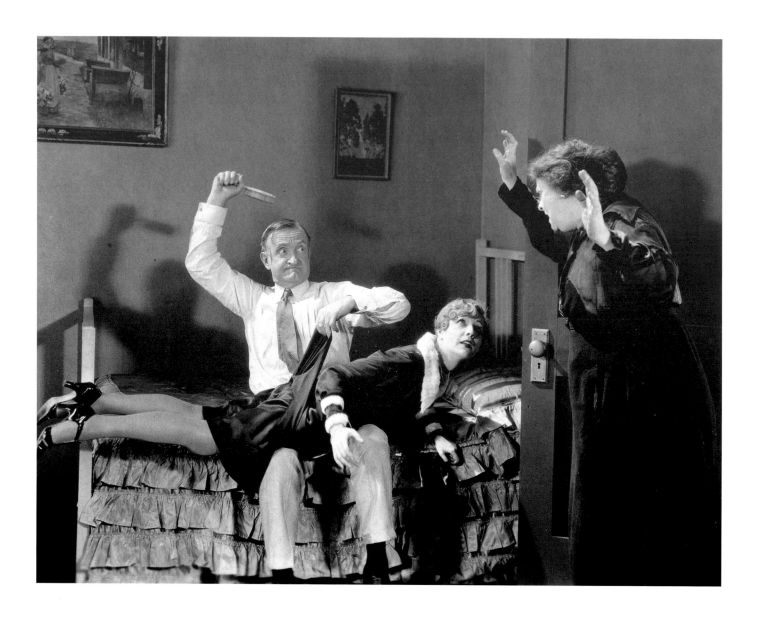

Dan McFadden (Charlie Murray), an Irish hod-carrier who becomes a building contractor, builds McFadden's Flats and becomes a millionaire. Having acquired his wealth, McFadden sends his daughter, Mary Ellen (Edna Murphy, centre), to a finishing school. Her changed ways, including abandoning her Scottish boyfriend Sandy for the upper class flapper lifestyle, makes her father angry, and to the horror of Mrs McFadden (Aggie Herring, right), he beats his daughter. Eventually, Mary and Sandy are reconciled.

In EASY COME, EASY GO, Martin L Donovan (Barry Fitzgerald, centre) combines worrying about the success of the horses he bets on with his opposition to his daughter Connie's (Diana Lynn) relationship with Kevin O'Connor (Sonny Tufts), or with anyone else.

HOME IS THE HERO

(Fielder Cook, Ireland, 1959, b&w)

On his return from jail, Paddo O'Reilly (Walter Macken, left) is confronted by his son Willie (Arthur Kennedy) who, in his father's absence, has usurped his position as head of the family. Paddo's wife, Daylia (Eileen Crowe) is a bystander to the struggle between father and son. Walter Macken's performance in the adaptation of his own play was praised by contemporary reviewers.

James T Farrell's *Studs Lonigan* trilogy was a milestone in Irish-American literature when it was published in the 1930s. Its adaptation as a feature film was less enthusiastically received, but it retained as a central theme the struggle within the family between the authoritarian father, Patrick Lonigan (Dick Foran, right), and his son, Studs (Christopher Knight), while Mrs Lonigan (Katherine Squire) is trapped between the two men.

LE PURITAN

(Jeff Musso, France, 1937, b&w)

The first feature film made about the sexual repression of the Irish was made in France, not Ireland. In this adaptation of Liam O'Flaherty's novel, a young journalist, Francis Ferriter (Jean-Louis Barrault, above), who is a member of a vigilance society, has rigid and conservative moral attitudes, and is frightened of women. He murders a woman because he regards her as immoral. Haunted by the crime, Ferriter confesses it to a priest, who refuses to absolve him of his guilt. He wanders in the low parts of town where he befriends a prostitute to whom he admits the crime. Later, Ferriter confesses to the police, claiming he really loved the woman he killed.

By the 1960s, the role of institutional Catholicism in reinforcing sexual repression had come under cinematic scrutiny. In I CAN'T... I CAN'T..., a young Dublin woman, Mady (Tessa Wyatt), fears getting pregnant when her mother dies after a miscarriage. Mady's fear continues after her marriage to Joe O'Reilly (Dennis Waterman), but when she seeks counsel from Father Keegan (Martin Dempsey) she is told repeatedly that the Catholic Church prohibits 'artificial' contraception. Unable to see a way out of her dilemma, she attempts suicide.

I WAS HAPPY HERE

(Desmond Davis, GB, 1965, b&w)

Cass Langdon (Sarah Miles) leaves London and her English husband, Dr Matthew Langdon, to return to her native County Clare where she remembers an earlier time of happiness with Colin Foley (Sean Caffrey). Matthew follows her to Ireland, but he returns home alone.

Breaking the taboos of her Protestant community, servant Sarah (Saskia Reeves) has children by her two employers, Frank Echlin (Ciaran Hinds, left) and his brother Hamilton (Donal McCann). Despite local pressures, she refuses to marry either of them until her children grow up and they want to normalise their social status.

HUSH-A-BYE BABY

(Margo Harkin, Ireland, 1989, colour)

Against a background of the war in Northern Ireland in the 1980s and the divisive referendum on abortion in the Republic, Derry teenager Gorett (Emer McCourt) becomes pregnant, but her boyfriend is jailed on alleged terrorist offences. Afraid to reveal her pregnancy to her parents, Goretti struggles to come to terms with her future.

Incest victim Angela Devine (played by non-professional, real-life traveller Judy Donovan) marries fellow traveller Michael Connors (Davy Spillane). During the course of a journey from the Republic to Northern Ireland, Angela reveals her father's violent and abusive attacks on her. Angela's increased self-awareness leads to the realisation that her future lies outside Ireland.

DAUGHTER OF DARKNESS

(Lance Comfort, GB, 1947, b&w)

Priest's housekeeper Emmy Baudine (Siobhan McKenna) turns her back on religion in the person of her employer, Father Corcoran (Liam Redmond), as she tries to come to terms with the mesmerising effect she has on men. After Father Corcoran sends Emmy to Yorkshire in response to pressure from his Irish parishioners, she kills three men there. When her responsibility for the murders is uncovered, her employer forces her out on the moors where a wailing dog belonging to one of her victims attacks her.

While fantasising about life on a South Pacific island, work-shy Irish civil servant Gulliver Shiels (Robert Beatty), who hasn't been to work for eighteen months, meets Jennifer Stockley (Moira Lister). She becomes determined to re-orientate his fantasy towards a more conventional lifestyle of marriage and work.

WINGS OF THE MORNING

(Harold D Schuster, GB, 1937, colour)

Disguised as 'Don Mario', Irish-Spanish gypsy Maria (Annabella) escapes to Ireland during the Spanish Civil War. Maria shares a haybarn with Canadian Kerry Gilfallen (Henry Fonda) during a storm. As they become attracted to each other, and to Kerry's relief, 'Don Mario' turns out to be a woman.

IRA killer Jude (Miranda Richardson, seated) is even more confused when she finds herself in competition with Dil (Jaye Davidson, standing), the trans-sexual male lover of both her ex-boyfriend, Fergus, and of the black British soldier she entrapped.

INDEX

Film titles, directors and
actors appearing in the stills
are included in the index.

George Sidney and Mack Swain in
THE COHENS AND THE KELLYS IN ATLANTIC CITY
(William James Craft, USA, 1929)